To Andy

RAMBLINGS OF A ONE-EYED GARBAGE MAN

BY JIM HART

Copyright © 2013 Jim Hart
All rights reserved.

ISBN: 1480125865
ISBN-13: 9781480125865
Library of Congress Control Number: 2012919669

CreateSpace Independent Publishing Platform
North Charleston, South Carolina

For Sue, Chris and Ali ... for being them.

Cover Photograph by Chris Hart

ACKNOWLEDGMENTS

Many of the poems collected here first appeared in the following publications:

The Aurorean: "Harry Taylor"
The Blind Man's Rainbow: "Joe-Annmarie And Oui Three"
Caveat Lector: "Funny Man"
Epicenter: "And The 72 Virgins Weren't Saving Themselves For You Either"
Haight Ashbury Literary Journal: "Dream: For Two"
The Iconoclast: "Deadwood"
Illumen: "Hiroshima Cloud Cover"
Nerve Cowboy: "February 20, 1957 - August 4, 1982"
Namad's Choir: "Bitter Cold"
Pegasus: "Angrily Rakes The Saturday Afternoon Boy Of Summer"
Poetry Depth Quarterly: "In Minor Keys"
Poetry Salzburg Review (Austria): "Leaps Of Faith"
The Poet's Pen: "Amen"
Pulsar (England): "Eddie Malone - Teenage Pilot"
Quantum Leap: "Stormy"
Red Owl Magazine: "Freedom"
River Poet's Journal: "Greenwich Village - 1967"
Shemom: "Mother's Lessons"
Waterways: "Nutritional Facts Not On The Label"
Taj Mahal Review: "Motherload"

CONTENTS

RAMBLINGS 1

Replay 2
Amen 4
Family Tree 6
Greenwich Village - 1967 7
A Questionable Youth 8
In Loving Memory 10
Mother Load 12
February 20, 1957 - August 4, 1982 14
Eddie Malone - Teenage Pilot 15
The Night I Learned To Play Darts 16
Funny Man 18
Fallen - On Deaf Ears 19
The Locksmith And The Salesgirl 20
Fading With The Night 22
Bitter Cold 24
Dead Letter Drop 25
A Thorny Issue 26
A Shade Too Late 28
...And Then It All Goes Black 30
And the 72 Virgins Weren't Saving Themselves For You Either ... 32
Leaps Of Faith 34
Give John Enough Rope 35
Old Fashioned Prices 36
Tempo 38
Ambition Ambush 40
To Be Half The Man 42
The Eight-Year Old 1950's TV Writer 43

Pink Oil Mammography 44
The Gowanus Boys Of Subterfuge 45
Grizzly 46

FREE 47

Indistinct Perspectives 48
Between Two Perfect Trees 49
Always First Perfections. 50
Summer Dreams 51
Joe-Annmarie and Oui Three 52
Mother's Lessons 53
Freedom 54
Empty Sleeping Bag 56
End Without End 58
Luna Tick 59
Pulled Back Sheet 60
Dream: For Two 61
Acid Trip 62
Reminiscence Of A Cold Winter Night 64
Hiroshima Cloud Cover 66
Stormy 68
Deadwood 69
Angrily Rakes The Saturday Afternoon Boy Of Summer 70
1951 Heart Transplant 72
Uninspired By The New - Creakless Floors 74
Non-Fighter Pilot 75
Rhyme-Meter 76

BURSTS 77

Cream Cheese And Jelly On Toast
Cut Triangularly In Quarters 78
Propinquity 79
In Our Garden 80

Again	81
Well Aligned	82
Harry Taylor	83
"To...	84
In Minor Keys	85
Powder Blue Walls Stenciled With The Classics	86
My Father Lowered All Her Kitchen Cabinets	87
Delicate Balance	88
Rough Sketch	89
Processions	90
Homecoming	91
Another Viet Casualty	92
Neglectful	93
Aunt Kay's Sin	94
At This Age It's More A Matter Of Me Needing My Sleep	95
Artisan	96
Conductor	97
Clean Underwear Made No Difference	98
For Crying Out Loud	99
Out Of Focus	100
A Feast	101
Three Critics	102
One-Pound Ground	103
Athletic Prowess	104
Nutritional Facts Not On The Label	105
So It's Come To This	106
It's Late - His Father Will Kill Him	107

RAMBLINGS

REPLAY

The night becomes long with Love gone. The blackness turns eternal and distant cat meowing – sounds like amplified rock groups turned up to ten. Nervous energy does all the chores that have backed up over the last three months by 9:30 – and TV becomes some not too well liked neighbors out of focus vacation slide show stuck at twenty minute intervals with minute detail descriptions – "See that rock – the big one – third from the left – Little Jenny skinned her knee on that one".

He did not want to face another night alone – yet there was no one he wanted to be with – now that Love was gone.

He stared in the mirror long and hard - not moving – as if he were watching some childhood double feature at the corner movie house – he could have gone for popcorn – there were no lines in the lobby – but was too into the picture of his own life staring back at him from behind the bathroom sink. He had left the light off when he went in – he never bothered to put it on – he knew where everything was – this now added to the Bijou feeling of groping for a seat – though he did not have to grope nor was he seated.

He watched the movie closely – Love was in it. She had the starring role – with many close ups – and spoke in that soft sweet voice of their first meeting. She was saying – "I can't bear to live without you" for the third time as the camera zoomed to an extra tight shot of her moist pouty lips – but the music rose slightly - a sure sign there is trouble ahead for these two – up till now – perfect lovers – a dead giveaway that she will all too soon learn that living without him can be the easiest thing in the world – she will in fact wonder why she did not live without him sooner.

He watched the movie closely – Love was exiting stage left for the fourth time tonight. This part always made him cry – no matter how many times he saw the movie – this part always made him cry.

Exhausted he fell asleep – for two whole hours he did not think of Love – he awoke in the bathtub to the sound of the telephone. He jumped up hopping it was Love – it was his mother asking him how he was – she hadn't heard from him in a long time and she was worried.

"I'm fine,"

                      he lied.

AMEN

Irish wakes
At least the ones I've attended
Are more about food than drink

Perhaps
Like most of civilization
the Irish have mellowed
and the "common perception" (<u>stereotype</u>)
was once true
And the drinking went on
into the night
And sorrows
if not drowned
were temporarily immersed
in forgetful imbibement

So What!

Do Italian
    Black
and Spanish women scream too loud
at their husbands coffin side

Do Asians sit too peacefully
to truly be feeling sorrow

We all hurt in our own way
And more so as individuals
than races

Leave it alone

Don't analyze it

Be happy
that this time
it's not your pain.

FAMILY TREE

She polished daily
the flightless from living room butterfly table
From 1936 wedding year
until her eighty year old death
As religiously as her Sunday Catholic communion
she Pledged her mahogany sheen
Removing lamp and doily
and occasional husband left book
humming happily in joyous chore well done
Shining site of first thing seen through doorway
reflected off dark green leather chair
and in pride of mother's eyes
Removed now
to my - two doors down dining room corner place of honor
Rubbed not with her vigor
but with the tender wistful feeling
that it is a sacred wood
carved from the outstretched branches of her love

GREENWICH VILLAGE – 1967

We were talking about distance – logistics – how hard no car dating was - and more deeply about her desire for other men in her life. We were by a big window in a coffee shop and outside – between looks at each other – we noticed the snow was falling just beyond our words. She loved me – she declared just loud enough for each uniquely shaped flake to hear – but there was Dennis and Roy and somebody else whose unimportant name I've forgotten – and she loved them too.

"Hey, the fleet's in," I said, "there must be a coupla guys you missed from last time."

It was cruel – overly cruel – but I was young and hurting. How could she spread her love around so freely. How could she love us all – and the others who had come before. There would – of course – be more to come – but I was having too much trouble dealing with the present to worry about any future – especially one I was rapidly realizing – only seconds after the joy of hearing her say she loved me – would no longer include me

A QUESTIONABLE YOUTH

The house of my youth floats easily through my dreams
Four brothers at play/war
Mom and Dad in various stages/rages of love
Report card days were most upsetting – for me

Running out the door and down the walled stoop
Always a game of punch-foot-basket or baseball waiting
Assigned TV nights meant to avoid fights
That forgotten – "I traded you's" – got in the way of
Dad's invention of micro-surgery
If there were two of us and one piece of cake – "One guy cuts – the other guy picks."
God how perfectly even my one eye learned to find dead center

Mom and her old washing machine
Passing shirts – pants and everything else through a wringer into a tub
To be carried out the backdoor to the clothesline
The small black and white TV given by Aunt Kay for Joe's tenth (I was two) birthday
Running from the vacant lot ball field to be in by five p m
To watch the had-a-crush-on Annette Mickey Mouse Club
With its different – Adventure – Talent – Roundup – etc, Days

Start of the summer "peach fuzz days" – named for JoJo, Alleyboy and their cousin Al
Who's grandfather had been a barber and gave them school's over baldy haircuts every year

1958 – My Brother John – and the summer of my discontent

"Hey, you – you friggin' nigger!" – Peppy Infanti – the Italian
punk from down the block called me
I asked John what a nigger was
Go ask Dad – he said
Pow! – Never say that again – My father responded

"Hey, punk - how come you got your balls all twisted?" – Joey
Bannorra said.
I asked John what my balls were
Go ask Dad – he said
Pow! – Never say that again – The old man was nothing if not
consistent

John told me to go ask Joe – the Jewish guy who owned the
paper-stand why he had his telephone number tattooed on his
arm.
Pow! – Joe responded
I told my father Joe had hit me
Come with me he said with that Irish peer in his eyes – and I
knew Joe was dead meat
Did you say anything to him – he asked on the way to Joe's
No – I said – I just asked him why he had his telephone number
tattooed on his arm
Pow! – The walk to Joe's ended

You think – even at only eight years old – I'd have learned
something about my brother John – wouldn't you?

IN LOVING MEMORY

My monsters
were never under the bed
or in the closet
or
unfortunately
imagined

They were the real moans
of my dying Aunt Kay's
next bed room
cancer stricken pain

I was seven
young enough
not to know the full extent of her condition
old enough
to sniff its fear

MOTHER LOAD

She reads the telegram
bearing the weight of its words
in two hands

A single sheet of paper
heaver than Atlas could support

She need read no further than
"It is with the deepest regret . . ."

In fact
she knew
    upon seeing the emboldened eagle
    top of letterhead embossed
that John
  her only son
  was gone

"It is with the deepest regret . . ."

She read out loud
making the words come true
making them her own
not merely some dictated statement of fact

Making them somehow heavier
riding on air

Her hands fell to her sides
her sides were somehow seated in the old porch swing
its rusty chains echoing the weeping of her heart

"It is with the deepest regret . . ."
   deepest regret
   deepest regret
      the swing repeated over and over
      until darkness robbed the words
      from the page by her side
      the words she never spoke again

FEBRUARY 20, 1957 – AUGUST 4, 1982

    He sets the bottle down easy and slow – the kind of slow that says the bottle is already half empty – searching for right depth to let go – the kind of slow that says there was a table around here someplace – and not that long ago – the kind of slow that slides through the little ringlets of put down before like a commercial airliner making a full passenger wheel-less emergency landing on a pre-foamed highway in the middle of a Nebraska late August night – where even the well traveled stewardesses have used to capacity their air sick bags – and the captain screams "Jesus – Fuckin – Christ" into the loud speaker like a well written psalm of perfect expression – extracting more heartfelt A Men's' than Billy Graham has ever heard in all his years on the holy Bible Belt campaign trail – and the slick synthetic tarpaulin rolls out the door to form a perfect chute as one by one they slide to their safety like fleet footed baseball men stealing second – no throw from the catcher – a hundred and forty seven thumbs strung out on the great American interstate like a flag waving in the golden wheat horizon – waiting for a Buick pick up in a dyna flow dream

    He sets the bottle down easy and slow – the kind of slow that says he will be just that much too late in going from gas to break on the winding road back home

    His friends stare at him easy and slow – the kind of slow that says they are not going to try to stop him

JIM HART

EDDIE MALONE – TEENAGE PILOT

He threw more than his life out that window

Back so many years ago

What about those who could've/should've been born to him

He was smarter than most of the guys we hung with

Maybe than all of 'em

He was sure as hell smarter than me

But he kept buying airplane models

And never fitting the pieces together

Just sniffing the glue long enough

I guess

Will make even the smartest of guys think he can fly

THE NIGHT I LEARNED TO PLAY DARTS

There's a dart game going on – in the corner – the back right corner – of this Fourth Avenue, Brooklyn bar. I don't know how to play darts. It's not all – just aim for the bull's-eye – there's a scoring system – with so many of these – and so many inside the narrow rings – and a bunch of shit like that – but eight beers into the slowly turning night I decide I'm up for the challenge. Never mind not knowing the rules – that's the least of my worry – my main concern should be – but never has been – I've only one eye – and so hampered not only by the distortion of eight beers and not knowing the rules – I have no depth perception – and guess the distance of my first few shots with much laughed at – right of target deployment.

After a reasonable amount of time I find it's like passing double parked cars – a trait I went at with not as much fervor or enthusiasm – thankfully for my insurance rates – and ease to within the odd hundred points or so of my opponent – who is just now bothering to mention – to the sardonic smiles of his cohorts – that the standard fare in this neck of the woods is a dollar a point – I smile the same jackal-like grin of his pack and announce with much panache that the next round is on me.

I take the empties from the stool and from the hands of two jackal friends and bring them to the bar – returning with only two – still tightly capped – one for each hand – and start my wind milling assault that takes no more than a few minutes.

Retrieving the wallet of the head jackal I empty it of its more than likely ill-gotten green folding gains – pay the bartender – with enough of a tip to keep his fingers off the phone – and still have plenty to blow on a cab ride home – explaining to my brother Jerry that darts is not such a tough game – once you learn how to take aim.

FUNNY MAN

I thought about it

Thought about it just that much longer and two beers more than I should have

It always seems to go that way

Just that little bit more that pushes me over the edge

I went out my door and knocked on his

"You Charlie?" I asked – Hell demanded

"Yeah – dickwad," he smiled

It was that kind of smile that guys whose abilities usually run fifteen percent short of their confidence levels wear

I hit him with everything I had and watched him tumble back into his living room

Then borrowed his smile for the walk back to my place

JIM HART

FALLEN – ON DEAF EARS

She's a latchkey kid
Parents divorced
Their lives fucked up
why not hers
They're certainly too self-centered
to care
One off to Bermuda for the weekend
the other at *the mountain place*
getaway retreat with the lover
Neither bothering to check in
while the police frantically search
address books and work contacts
making call after call
in a futile effort to notify someone
their daughter lies dead in the kitchen
having trusted that little chain lock gizmo
would protect her
from a two hundred and thirty pound pervert
who wanted
desperately
to taste her so young flesh

THE LOCKSMITH AND THE SALESGIRL

She only had to give her Avon saleslady-smile once – from his third floor hall – to capture forever the dream of the first sweet touching of their mouths.

When her smile faded into words he thought his heart had stopped – He did not hear what she was saying – he was too busy watching her mouth for some signal – no matter how faint – that her smile was about to return – to reappear in mid sentence – stopping her flow of murderous words with the reprieve of her slightly parted lips.

She waited for him to answer – but he had heard nothing – and stunned back to reality by her silence – or rather by the non movement of her mouth – he fumbled like a schoolboy caught daydreaming by the wise old teacher who had learned to recognize in boys the far off look on first Spring mornings that says "There are no answers in my mind today – there are only questions – questions that have nothing to do with classrooms – or books or old prodding teachers who have forgotten love long before I was born."

But she is waiting for him to speak so he says "You have a beautiful smile – can I see it again?"

This makes her laugh – her laugh makes her smile look like a cold Siberian winter morning on a frozen plain – and he asks her in so he may better look at her catalogue of exotic smelling after shaves in Mail Box – Antique Car – Capitol Building shaped bottles with "He Man" names like *Wild Country* and *Wind Jammer.*

FADING WITH THE NIGHT

He ripped the note to tiny pieces – It was her note – Her goodbye note – He did not want to see again the part about how much she did not love him anymore – He kept seeing it over and over – He had ripped the note up – But he could not erase the "I don't love you" from in front of his eyes – It stared back at him for hours like some 1963 blue dot flash cube stenciled on his pupils

I don't love you

I don't love you

I don't love you showed up wherever he looked – He tried to imagine her now – Coolly walking about the house – Watering the plants – Having pleasant little conversations on the phone with the girls – Watching the afternoon soaps

He began to breath heavy – his hands got sweaty – He got dizzy and fell back on the couch - Closing his eyes to two side by side I don't love you   I don't love you's brightened by the darkness of background inner lids

The room was total darkness when his sight returned to normal – He tried to read the note as it lay in a hundred pieces on the floor – Maybe he had read it wrong – Sure – maybe it was "I love you more and more" – Her penmanship would never win any awards and he had read the note without his glasses – Maybe she was home right now waiting for his call – Wondering what was wrong – He dialed her 546-9464 number and felt that old familiar pain as a man's voice said "Hello-Hello who is this

– If this is you Jim she doesn't want to see you anymore – Didn't you get her note" – He pressed the little button gently down then placed the receiver back on its cradle

He believed it now – No more sweaty palms – No more heavy breathing – Just an ever so slight
                                        I don't love you anymore – blue ink on yellow legal paper – Fading with the night

BITTER COLD
1978

Oh Russia
    Russia of frozen snow
        of frozen people
           living day to day
           warmed only by your vodka

    Russia of machine like loyalty
        of one party lines
           where only banished poets
           speak in truths

    Russia of Kremlin like buildings
        of Red Squares
           where hard working comrades cheer
           military weapons

    Russia of Lenin was bad
        Stalin was bad
        Krucheiv was bad
        cowardice denunciations

    Russia of Hitler hatred
            How can you curse the Jews
            Have you learned nothing
            from icy fingered invaders
            knocking at your door
            cold December mornings
            rifles in their hands?

DEAD LETTER DROP
7/5/05

The mailman delivers a strange letter
Stamped with a green three cent likeness of George Washington
and a purple Postage Due

The letter is from my cousin, Frank
killed in World War II

A hero – charging machinegun nest

It is addressed to me
at my current residence

Double strangeness
as I was not yet born when Frank was cut in two by a fifty caliber
and naturally
did not live at this address

I pay the thirty-six cents owed
and begin to read – door still open to the passing world of 64th street
that Frank is fine – and we – the family – should not be concerned
He's quite sure he'll be home for Christmas
If not this one
Then certainly the next

A THORNY ISSUE

Did the other kids resent Jesus
the child at play
Were they envious
that all his wooden animals
were carved with such perfection
that they walked
or flew away
Were they angered
that his sailboats in puddles
carried real fisherman
with fish full nets
to always needy markets
Did they hate him
his always
"Yes Mother"
goodness
never needing
second time calling
or first time explanation
How hard it must have been
for all of them
when mothers
as mothers through the ages do
drew the
must have drawn
"Why can't you be more like Jesus?"
comparisons

You think
that might have had something to do
with why
latter on in life
when cross came to bare
there were no Jews
for Jesus

A SHADE TOO LATE

My Aunt Maude's house was in the West Streets just off Brooklyn's Highlawn Avenue. She - as most of my relatives – was very old when I was very young. Nobody names their daughters Maude anymore. I don't directly connect this fact to my aunt – because even if she had been the worst person in the world – which she wasn't – not everybody could have met her and based their no Maude naming decision solely on her personality.

BUT – she did used to pull the shades down on her windows and sit as quiet as the old church mouse she would eventually become when my young boy father rode his bike over to visit her. This was actually pretty ironic because in those later years he was – as usual – the one to visit and help her the most.

To be absolutely fair to Aunt Maude – my father was more like his four sons than his two half-brothers – well one of them anyway – and there were probably plenty of people who made believe they weren't home when he came to visit. Hey, there were probably a bunch who went the extra yard and actually went out just to avoid the shoot-the-heads-off-roses-with-a-bee-bee-gun little hellion.

Anyway – I remember Sunday visits – my father picking – near the end – colostomy bagged Aunt Maude off the couch and carrying her upstairs for Aunt Lotti – another name thankfully ignored by present day parents – to give her a proper washing and grooming. My father cleaning up in the house and assigning us - *yard work*.

Once – before she got sick – my father, brother Jerry and I were visiting. Aunt Maude went shopping and asked my father to prune one of the trees in her yard while she was gone. He got the ladder and some big old tree branch cutting saw and climbed up into the tree. Jerry and I shot hoops – perhaps missed hoops would be a more accurate description – in the basket over the garage doors. My father hit the ground with a thud. We ran to him scared as hell – never having seen our father fall out of a tree before and not knowing what to expect. He stood up slowly and told us not to say a word about it. Especially to Mom or Aunt Maude. About five minutes later she came walking into the yard pulling her groceries in a cart behind her. My father looked at her and said, "Maude, I just fell out of your tree."

Jerry and I were amazed! Aunt Maude took the groceries in the back door - and I got the very strong feeling that if she hadn't just spoken with us - she would have pulled the shade down and pretended she wasn't home.

... AND THEN IT ALL GOES BLACK

Your sugar levels are all over the map
the doctor says without looking up from the report on his desk
He looks concerned
His eyes are traveling my blood sugar roads
Back and forth
Up and down
From Brooklyn to San Francisco
From Seattle to Texas
He is scanning in heightened alarm
Route 465
is evidently *not*
a good road for sugar haulers
And now
unbeknownst to him
my blood pressure
has latched on to my sugar level
like an expert hitchhiker
along for the heart pounding
head aching ride
And I am changing lanes
and gears like a drunken sailor
rushing after eight months sea duty
to be by the side of his
sexually starved girlfriend
and then ...

AND THE 72 VIRGINS WEREN'T SAVING THEMSELVES FOR YOU EITHER

He believes Heaven
is anything you want
you can do anything you ever wanted to
by gaining admittance

I mean
suppose you always wanted
to break All the commandments

But you didn't
Because
you wanted to get to Heaven

So now you're floating on a cloud
and you see a guy you know
and hated

I mean he stole your job
        your wife
        your kids
        your life

So POW
you shoot him
with the gun that magically
maybe even miraculously appeared in your hand

Because
you always wanted to give him one
right in the head

Even assuming
he was the biggest A-hole
in the world
he somehow got to Heaven
and I can't imagine
even for one minute
that his dream scenario
was catching one
right between the baby blues
from a bum like you
who couldn't even hold on to a job

LEAPS OF FAITH

When the air raid sirens rang

We hid – obediently – under our desks

Protected from Atomic Bomb blasts

By kindling wood and un-shattering beliefs

Watched over by nuns of stronger faith

Standing – habited – at front of room

Monitoring the diligence of our movements

As the honesty of our test taking

Leading us in prayer

And pledges of allegiance

Not noticing or caring

How our little bodies shook

It was one of the few un-pleasantries

Of the peaceful 1950's

And except for the day Johnny Iannonni wet his pants

We took it pretty well

GIVE JOHN ENOUGH ROPE

When we were young
my brothers and I
we found a dead cricket
(I still think John killed it)
But we got one of my father's little boxes
from his basement workroom
and being the good Christian boys we were
(maybe minus one cricket murderer)
we put the cricket in
and gave him a Christian burial
John (probably through guilty conscience)
wrote on the box
                "Here lies Jiminy Cricket"
and we started to say a prayer
stopping quickly after just Hailing Mary
Remembering our Catholic upbringing
and that only people had souls
and figuring that if you weren't even supposed to pray for a dead dog
you certainly shouldn't pray for a dead cricket
But we buried him
right and proper
scooped the dirt in
taking sad – bereaved turns with one of Mom's kitchen spoons
Did all we could
Except maybe John – who fancy lettering and all
couldn't quite hide the smirk
that to this day let me know
Jiminy didn't really hang himself from Mom's rosebush

OLD FASHIONED PRICES
(November 1981)

      Burma Shave   .69cent Sale

Burma Shave!   They still make Burma Shave? I had seen it only in a 1945 back issue of "Life" - glanced at in the second-hand bookstore sort of way – and had naturally assumed it had gone the way of the World War II forgotten warriors – dropped from the drug store shelves as thoroughly and suddenly as the atom bomb hit Hiroshima.

    Even now seeing sale sign in Pink Day Glo '80's approach to bargain basement inducements – I see Dick Powell sort as mercenary - holed up in cheap hotel room in black and white movie Algiers – with a thin mustached greasy little man behind the bar downstairs and a four blade fan spinning languidly on the ceiling.

    Dick lifts his right arm – straight razor about to touch face – when in the mirror we see the door to his room open and the long barrel of a black heater make its entrance. Dick smiles and very un-'80's like carefully places the razor on the sink and prepares to do battle the long gone brave bare fisted way – eight full celluloid tough fighting – three bad guys disposed of minutes later he returns to sink – fresh lit "Lucky" danglin' from his lips – razor back in hand – lather still thick on both cheeks.

TEMPO

In her dreams she was the lady of his song and she pictured him dancing around on the bare wood floor of the apartment holding her framed picture to his breast as he wide smile glided – sometimes holding her at arm›s length – staring breathless into her portrait eyes.

He was big and clumsy always stumbling over things – even in familiar surroundings – but in her dreams he moved like Astaire – up steps – over pianos – completely vaulting the bed – landing with picture perfect grace – legs crossed – hand on chin in the tufted Wing backed chair in the corner.

He was in fact thinking of her at this very moment – Thinking of how to drop – The I Don't Love You Anymore – H bomb – he had been inventing in the early morning hour dreams of his own.

He had been conducting secret dream tests – for about fourteen months – in the Nevada desert – meeting sultry slender scientists with foreign accidents and mathematical equations – Proof Positive – of his dying love.

They would awake one Saturday morning to the same harsh realized – After the kids – After the mortgage – After the car payments – After the orthodontist – After the too old to start again – too late – I never really loved you reality – and merely decide to be civil to each other 'till the day at 63 he keeled over at the kitchen table into a bowl of Corn Flakes – and she – too tired to care anymore about appearances sake – let him soak until the emergency medical unit arrived – some hour and a half later – and plunked his albino prune face down on the table with a thud that shook her dream memories alive – and she cried as once again he floated across bare wood floors to the deep stirred feelings of her young woman's heart.

AMBITION AMBUSH

Once
    Before you became a walking mannequin for ostentatious "Designer" attire
    Before you wore a hired smile painted on your billboard lips as false and long lasting as a portrait
    Before you could store - un-melted - snowflakes in your mouth
    Before the mirror practiced to perfection art of meaningless expression
    Before your lies sprang like truths in the midst of your deceptive beguilement
    Before carrying the world's ambition on your leaned back - squared off shoulders
    Before becoming a seller of illusions to lusting men and wanna-be beautiful women
    Before sporting a lift-up bra and a letdown personality

There
    was
        Us

    Do you miss me - even in the wounds of your unhealed dreams
    Do you miss the way night hung like a shutter against our well lit love
    Do you miss the touch of my lips you swore then - as forever - first
    Do you miss the breathing desire of love's lighted fire
    Do you miss your head morning nestled in my crooked arm

Do you miss the taste of compassionate attention
Do you miss the priceless moments of us - alone
Do you miss the how - the why - the if

Do you miss
        even a little
                Us

TO BE HALF THE MAN

We were watchers – mostly
when it came to the house
my brothers and I
Watched my father wire new outlets
Watched him measure – saw – replace
whatever age wore – bent crooked – or warped out of line
Watched tubes go in and out of radios and TV's
with under-breath hoping before final joy
Watched the plum lines snapped for tile laying floors
Watched the lead – Mom's stove top melted
to be poured into coffee can mold weights
Watched the radiators drained to gain new valves
Watched the under sink pipes get replaced
Watched the chessmen soldered into nut and bolt armies
of good design and better battlefield strategies
Watched as the same kneel – stand – sit – kneel – stand – kneel
rigidity
he followed at every Sunday Mass
coursed through his tutorial veins
until his boys gave way to men
Watched as he hung on
floating between reality and that place where mixed-up
mugged beaten heads dwell
until he was sure
his job was done

JIM HART

THE EIGHT-YEAR OLD 1950'S TV WRITER

He sat in green leather rocker – feet on the hassock – library book lit by the yellow shaded floor lamp standing in the corner behind the left hand side of his chair. Many a night he'd fall asleep like that – Woodhouse's Jeeves – towel over one arm – bowing slightly at the waist – leading him to gentle slumber. Short – combed straight back hair showing the faintest signs of grey – Mom – taking the open book from his stomach and piece of paper or matchbook cover marking page – laying it on the small – well polished – butterfly table by his side – then signaling us to lower the old black and white TV's volume. I think it was nights like these that helped me learn to write – having to fill in my own dialogue every time a train went by – usually at a crucial, dramatic moment – drowning out the most important part of whatever the heck I was watching. I was secretly happy – although I'd complain – quietly – to mom that I was missing all the good parts – because my brothers complained and at that age you follow the older guys lead. But in my mind – regardless of their movements on the screen – the characters said whatever I wanted them to. So that a detective merely pointing his finger and probably saying something like – "I have some questions for you" – became – "I swear – if I find out you're lyin' – and I have to come back here – this gun I'm pointin' at ya is just liable to add about an ounce of lead to your already too fat carcass."

PINK OIL MAMMOGRAPHY

She stared at the paintings hung on the walls

Trying to see past the canvas and oil

To the man

Pallet in hand

Stealing glances at his naked model

More concerned with capturing her spirit

Than her body

She takes a step back

Finally recognizing herself

By the slightly larger left breast captured to perfection

Which she has been daily monitoring in her bathroom mirror for months

And realizes at that very instant

That the lump is non-imagined

THE GOWANUS BOYS OF SUBTERFUGE

In the old days
The slow – turn of century days
Young boys would run along the canal
Cursing the coal-barge men
And giving them *the* finger

The men
Of natural turn-of-century reaction
Would throw lumps of coal at them
Which the boys would fight to retrieve

Their poor winter cold parents
Would laud their warmth stealing ways for days
Especially the skillful – unmarked dodgers
Who stood proudest basking in the glow

GRIZZLY

He sits
front porch
wicker rocking chair
The slow world of nature
creeping before him
like old Miss Crenshaw
making her way from her nephew Walter's car
to Miss Bailey's Hair Salon
every other Thursday
rain or shine
Night falling first
beyond the eastern tree tops
gradually taking over the field
raising him up
from his busy day
of arthritic whittling
of a marvelously detailed bear's head
that if he's lucky
will fetch five dollars
at the roadside flea market
where his daughter Jessica sells his work
to Yankee strangers
stopped by curiosity
on their way to *better* places

FREE

INDISTINCT PERSPECTIVES

What are clouds
beyond formations of our imagination

I see a face
    a castle
    a mountain fortress
        carved in rock

God
A sailing ship
A storm brewing in the northern quadrant
A sea of despair
An ex-lover
    moved on to happiness
        found
        only without me

What are clouds
but lies
told on stormy days
of blurred intentions
and unforgiving doubts

BETWEEN TWO PERFECT TREES

Just over
    the next street
        hangs the moon
            as lazy
                as an old man
                      in his hot afternoon
                          hammock

No swing
    in his
        open book on chest
             peaceful
                end of day

ALWAYS FIRST PERFECTIONS

Like the elongated shadows

        of summer

                sunny rain storms

                        she stretches

                              my belief in love

                                        with each new kiss

JIM HART

SUMMER DREAMS

Two old men

    Stick

    String

    Bubblegum

        fishing through

            the grate of memory

                for lost youth

JOE-ANNMARIE AND OUI THREE
9/29/01

We,
    the three uncles,
        take turns dancing
            with his wedding day daughter

Like
    some missing fighter-pilot formation
            of
                one-two-three
                  two-two-three
                we waltz through the dance
                  that should have been his.

JIM HART

MOTHER'S LESSONS

Teaching you to walk

    hands held high

        over head

The trusting smile

    as wide across your face

        as your step

Her gentle voice

    leading you

        from one end of the room

            to the rest of your life

FREEDOM

Sistered to each other

    as close as soul and shadow

They walk

    hand-in-hand

    down the proud street

        of too in love

            to give a damn

RAMBLINGS OF A ONE-EYED GARBAGE MAN

EMPTY SLEEPING BAG

Tortured with unknowing
   not taught with love
   the nine year old missing
                 found
                 raped
                 murdered
                       girl scout
   screams still crying
        in
        the
        woods
   wishes on little stars
            twinkling
            in
            the night
      forever unfulfilled
last visions
            of green pines
            in
            blue skies
blotted out
            by mad face
            back
               and
            forth
                rocking
  close
      then
          closer

'till she can see nothing
    save
    her own soul begging
            to be free

And
Tortured with unknowing
Earns no merit badge
    pinned
    to maroon sash

And
Nine-year old girl scouts
Cry forever
    in the forest

As
    constant reminders
        to
        animalistic
        tendencies
        that grow darker
           by
              the Night

END WITHOUT END

How little to lose
A Pay Check!
Oh, Dad
How I wish you'd made the choice
I know you couldn't
How I wish you'd let *them*
have it
How I wish I still had you
to talk to
to hold
to hug
to kiss once more on your rough whiskered cheek
Yes – even to suffer through your agony
                              forgetful
                                first time
                                          you needing me
                                                          years

Oh, Dad
How I wish you'd made the choice
I know you couldn't

LUNA TICK

The cloud passing before the moon

        in an eerie grey glow

        like hounds out on the moors

        or Big Ben sounding a cobblestone footfall alert

        or a back alley rapist

                waiting for your home late

                        shortcut taking

                              daughter

PULLED BACK SHEET

Midnight
> shadows the un-moon beamed buildings
> with the terror of the city streets

Dark
> chasms of hidden horrors
> waiting for your girlfriend/wife/daughter
> with murderous intentions
> that only you can protect them from

But you
> are sleeping

Waking only
> with the nightmare
> of completed deeds

You crawl slowly
> > to the police called to hospital
> > identifying officially
> > what you knew
> > before the ringing of the phone

JIM HART

DREAM: FOR TWO

Even a single rosebud blooming
    can seem ominous
        on this deep in returning from Church
            Sunday morning thoughts
                of her man off at war
                guns blaring through
                his other side of world night
                face split open
                by a Jap grenade

It is 1943
    she is 18
    and her unblossoming
        petals have wilted
    and her faith in God's
        been shattered
            through the deafness
                of His unanswering
                    prayer

And she takes her coke
        in double doses
        and trips off nightly
        to meet her Donald
        on some South Pacific Island
        where the sun is always setting
                as they walk naked
                    to the shore

ACID TRIP
(For Eddie – Summer 1968)

Plummeting

        from fifth floor window

        like water over Niagara

    shredding

        the air with his silence

    slicing

        the silence with his smile

    breaking

        the concrete with his fall

        and our hearts with his absence

REMINISCENCE OF A COLD WINTER NIGHT

Snow in the forest reminds me of war.

I was born in 1949.

Although I am a Roman Catholic – and cannot believe in reincarnation

I believe I died in battle.

The Battle of the Bulge.

No!

I don't believe I was

A General

A President

A Millionaire Industrialist

or great leader like everyone else

who believes themselves reincarnated does

I was

  as I am

      a simple man

And I don't remember specifics

              or friends

                      loved ones

                              or neighbors

I don't even remember being

I just remember dying

        in battle

        in the forest

        in the snow

                As frightened as a little boy

                As cold as hell

HIROSHIMA CLOUD COVER

The black rain fell
    and fell
        and in time
            they came to realize
                it was their friends and relatives
                    blasted into dust
                        raining down on them
                            for too many days
                                to count

        and they wiped them
                from their faces
        and breathed them in
                giving them back
                        bodies to live in

Until finally
        they didn't notice
            their falling particles
                dancing in the air
                and unnoticed
                      they stopped falling

        and life went on
                even with so many gone
        and the air cleared
        and the memory lifted
        and the white birds
                returned to the blue sky

JIM HART

    And an Emperor
        sat
        on a throne
            of Democracy

STORMY

You think it's romantic
        being married to a sailor
        because you never had to
                make love to a telegram
                from the South Seas
                    on a cold
                        moonless night

JIM HART

DEADWOOD

Winter high-wind storms

        clearing the trees

            of branches

                that can not

                      carry their own weight

RAMBLINGS OF A ONE-EYED GARBAGE MAN

ANGRILY RAKES THE SATURDAY AFTERNOON BOY OF SUMMER

Prongs

    spread across the lawn

        Like tigers teeth

            devouring a jaguar

1951 HEART TRANSPLANT

    We had

        on every year's

            Christmas tree

    A Santa Claus

        light bulb

           red – of course

    It was old

        when I was young

    And every year

        it would break

    And every year

        my father would go

        to throw it out

    And every year

        we would pester him

JIM HART

And every year

        he would take out his knife

        and run it along Santa's seams

        till he easily fell open

        and pliers gently

        remove his burnt out heart

        and pliers gently

            put a new one in

And every year

        Santa lit top of tree

And every year

        was 1951 red light miracles

        until my father died

        and Santa's heart burnt beyond repair

RAMBLINGS OF A ONE-EYED GARBAGE MAN

UNINSPIRED BY THE NEW – CREAKLESS FLOORS

Once again

    I walk the early morning halls

        of thoughts

           just beyond my grasp

        of ideas

          aborted

            instant of conception

       of poems

          laughing

            from behind

              their unwritten words

JIM HART

NON-FIGHTER PILOT

He stood

    on the eighteenth floor ledge

        as married to his decision

            as to his wife

                who's constant nagging

                    had driven him

                        to flight

RHYME RHYME RHYME
METER METER METER

My one eye
    averted from the book of poetry
        I was reading
            in the comfy-coffee-bar-chair
            by the big busy Avenue window

    to watch her poetry
        in motion
            summer afternoon
                short pants
                    saunter by

BURSTS

CREAM CHEESE AND JELLY ON TOAST CUT TRIANGULARLY IN QUARTERS

I wear my memories
like my mother her apron
Brought out not just for special occasions
but for every evening's meal
Washed
Worn
Mended
Tied forever
to our time together

JIM HART

PROPINQUITY

His electric razor

hummed on the porcelain sink long enough

to raise that subconscious fear

in her breakfast preparing mind

And in the instant

it took her to climb the stairs

his crash to tiled floor

echoed through her broken heart

IN OUR GARDEN
1964

We are standing
four boys
brothers
in black and white

The shadow
of our father
photographer
stretched across our beings

AGAIN

She kisses me goodbye
and I am once again
as unloved as an orphan
as lonely as a widow
cold winter's night
as unprepared for life
as a newborn baby
crying in my fear
and my unguarded naked shame

WELL ALIGNED
(For Joe Hart, Sr.)

He could measure
with bubble centered level accuracy
the true honesty
of just met men

HARRY TAYLOR
(District 31 — Sanitation - July 1975)

I really dig his head
from which
great musical vibes flow
he plays his words well
each picked for its single pitch
together making sentence song
whole paragraphs riffed off
with jazz like ease.

"TO...

the night Judy and I
made out on a stone bench
outside an 'Eternal Monument' store
never realizing
it was the death of our love."

JIM HART

IN MINOR KEYS
(For Elton John)

His music is the color of green traffic lights

Always in movement

Never crashing

Against the perfect pitch

Of his blue sky composure

POWDER BLUE WALLS STENCILED WITH THE CLASSICS

Her voice
a humming lullaby
to her unborn baby
Wanting him to sleep
before he is born
Wanting him to stop kicking
To kick more
letting her live the joy of pain
           the pain of joy
Unknowingly
she switches from Bach to Beethoven
and like a great Baldwin piano tree
her baby nestles in the branches
of her woman/mother body
And she smiles with the peaceful feeling
of his sheltered comfort
A liquid hammock
swaying lazily
in her unwomb room preparing day

MY FATHER LOWERED ALL HER KITCHEN CABINETS

Mrs. Robinson
the Manhattan wheelchair one
not the used to live next door one
was a sweet gentle woman
who smiled knowingly
at little boys wondering
what trapped inside a legless body was like

DELICATE BALANCE

Your fears
like thin ice
stretched out before you
waiting the exact weight
of conquest or defeat

The difference measured only
in the confidence or trepidation
of your first step

ROUGH SKETCH

The chalked outlines
of mob hit victims
imprint the Brooklyn streets
with young impressions
of what befalls
the squealer scum
that rats to cops
or Federal men
on anything
that happens
in the Borough of Churches

PROCESSIONS

The mourners
    flow past my mother's coffin
    like mid-night rivers
    overflowing onto low lying towns
    flooding basements
    washing away family photos and history's
    with generational disregard
    and trapping voluntary emergency rescuers
    in the sad bereavement of her passing's sorrow

HOMECOMING

Soldiers draped in country's flag
as if prideful symbols hadn't already done enough
as if parents hearts could soften to bugle's blare
as if any beyond those gathered truly cared
as if any even noticed beyond the **HEAD**lines to the story with your name
as if your high school girlfriend who you'd joined to impress ever noticed you were gone
as if the morning frost had not caught you drunk and drowsing on the job
as if you hadn't been clinging to survival at the thin edge of your murderers sardonic grin
as if you hadn't smelled your own flesh burning in the thick black air of atrocity
as if soldiers draped in country's flag were not more sad than heroic

ANOTHER VIET CASUALTY
1/10/98

She made love ONCE

A G.I. Joe or Flyboy

Some American uniformed hunk

And since 1972

Has been living with the round-eyed bastard son

Of every neighbors hatred

It's a small village

So there aren't many neighbors

But there's no number greater than EVERY

And at forty-four

With her son gone to seek his father

Accompanied only by the loneliness of no one who will talk to her

She puts her glasses on the table

And his gun in her mouth

JIM HART

NEGLECTFUL

Her tumor grows
like weeds in an untended garden
She could have hired a landscaper
or had those x-rays taken
back long ago
when there was still time
to trim the white-celled hedges
to untangle the leukemiaed ivy
from the thorny lymphatic roses
But only poets
and Englishmen
fall in love with perennials
she said
and who could live with either of them

AUNT KAY'S SIN
1957

Her voice comes muffled
from the ancient intercom
of my eight year old youth

The sounds of cancerous pain
forever unmasked
as the inescapable horror
of tumor pressing nerve
eating tissue and bone

Tempting you through torture
to drink the liquid morphine
Dr. Mendal left
beside your bed

AT THIS AGE IT'S MORE A MATTER OF ME NEEDING MY SLEEP

He calls her names
In a strange guttural language
I don't understand
But each name is accompanied
by a non-language barrier smack
that now has me knocking
(swore to Sue - though I did to mind my own effing business)
at their one apartment over - door
He's a big - young guy
with an already worked up Mean in his eyes
So the sucker punch for all I was worth
was not really as dirty a deed as it sounds
Especially when her pulped face came into view
with his falling

ARTISAN

He creates strange blurry shadows
like new backgrounds
in the lives of all the women he meets

He is quite creative

Chiseling away pasts
that don't include him

Carving away beliefs
inconsistent with those of his own

Picking – with dirty fingernail
the scars of previous lovers
until there is only the perfect complexion lie
of his vision

JIM HART

CONDUCTOR

His calloused fingers
vibrate the violin strings
to perfect pitch resonance

Beethoven, Bach, Brahms
cry like appreciative parents
in their non-composure coffins

He is six
and deaf
and feels each note
with a passion beyond Casanova's comprehension

He is six
and blind
and no one knows where the magic comes from
or where he goes when not playing
for he has never spoken a word

CLEAN UNDERWEAR MADE NO DIFFERENCE

The children of Pompeii
still play
beneath the molten rubble
I see them
stone Bocce balls in hands
One
about twelve
arm behind him
in that bowlers motion
has been dying to spin it lose
with young athletes skilled perfection
since ignoring his mother's shouting/pleading voice
to head for the sea

FOR CRYING OUT LOUD

You can love a person to death! She screams
I suppose implying suffocation
since our last physical encounter
wouldn't have over energized a gnat's heart
and occurred sometime in a warm month
and an odd numbered year
with an animal
the Chinese never thought of

OUT OF FOCUS

She wanted to project herself on me
As if I were a six-foot tall motion picture screen
And our life had been pre-scripted
By some high-priced Hollywood talent

The trouble was
I was a black and white '40's film noir
And she was a bright Techno Color bitch

JIM HART

A FEAST

The waitress laughs
scribbling her pad
with my hunger

It's a good laugh
worthy
of my appetite

So wide and filling
it leaves no room
for dessert

THREE CRITICS

At two-fifty-three A M
Precisely
Mary Todd Lincoln
was sitting up in her bed
describing to Abe
what the play they were going to see was about

She'd been telling him about it
for longer than the length of the play
Abe
ever the prophetic man
was wishing he were dead

ONE-POUND GROUND

The white butcher paper
of my youth
waxed by loving bees
seemed to carry less
artery clogging fat
than the pre-packaged
giant
uncaring
supermarket variety
killing us
in middle of street
heart stopping
face whacking ground
un-lean proportions
sold today

ATHLETIC PROWESS

The white chalk
flies past the well behaved
hitting only the wayward
daydreaming
lazy student

Such is the
"Sister of Saint Joseph" way

Each
hand picked
not only for intellectual ability
but for speed and accuracy
of their fast ball

NUTRITIONAL FACTS NOT ON THE LABEL

She refuses to eat – until he comes back she will starve herself thin – pretty – all the things he wants – wanted her to be – she will be through starvation.

I remind her of his stories of women left behind – of his bragging that his will was stronger than their won't – and ask – a bit sheepishly – how many dead women she thought there'd be – if all who came before her – had taken the same tact.

SO IT'S COME TO THIS

So it's come to this

A music box rendition of "Our Song"

Played in the darkness of a barely furnished room

Alone on North Charles Street

The seventy-three year old landlady

Knocking on the two A.M. door

With a bottle of twelve year old bourbon

And an ugly proposition

IT'S LATE – HIS FATHER WILL KILL HIM

At 3:00 A.M. he fits his key in the door

Like a doctor performing open heart surgery

An elderly woman polishes her family dining table each day with painstaking care. A man receives a long lost letter from an uncle killed in the line of duty. A young child creates his own imaginative dialogue to 1950s television shows. *Ramblings of a One-Eyed Garbage Man* is Jim Hart's collection of poetry that spans literary styles to capture an urban experience with profound social concern, sardonic wit, and a humorous perspective on the world that is certain to resonate with readers and thinkers everywhere.

Processing the world around him in an original yet uncomplicated way, Hart crafts poems that are at once pure, sweet, and raw, availing of multiple forms of verse to forge unique concepts for the everyman. Hart explores topics that draw from a certain time and place in the urban American experience, casting a searching eye on the depths and heights of humanity. Each work in *Ramblings of a One-Eyed Garbage Man* processes the past decades with fine perception, moral clarity, and palpable heart. Readers who value well-chosen words that are rich with life will treasure this graceful, enlightening collection.

ABOUT THE AUTHOR

JIM HART is an internationally published poet whose works have appeared in publications in the United States, Canada, England, Scotland, Austria, and India. He worked for the New York City Sanitation Department in positions including, Deputy Director of Public Affairs, and Director of Correspondence for the Sanitation Police/Enforcement Division. Hart was born and raised in Brooklyn, New York and currently lives there with his wife.

Made in the USA
San Bernardino, CA
30 April 2017